COLOMA PUBLIC LIBRARY

Junior Petkeeper's Library
MICE and RATS

Junior Petkeeper's Library

Mice and Rats

Fiona Henrie

Consultant Editor
Michael Findlay M.R.C.V.S.

Photographs by Marc Henrie A.S.C.

Franklin Watts
London New York Sydney Toronto 1980

Franklin Watts Limited
8 Cork Street
London W1

© 1980 Franklin Watts Limited

SBN UK edition: 85166 856 9
SBN US edition: 531 04187 5
Library of Congress Catalog Card No: 80 50484

Phototypeset by Tradespools Ltd, Frome, Somerset
Printed in Great Britain by
Tindal Press, Chelmsford, Essex

The publisher and author would like to thank the following
for their help in preparing this book: Eric Jukes of the National Mouse Club;
Chris McKnight; Nick Mayes; Roy Robinson, F. Biol.

Contents

Introduction	7
Choosing a mouse or rat	8
Preparing for your pet	10
Taking your pet home	13
Food	14
Hygiene	16
Activity	19
Handling	20
Breeding	22
Health and care	24
Shows	26
Varieties of mice	28
Varieties of rats	29
Checklist	30
Glossary	31
Index	32

Proper food and care will help to keep your pet in good condition.

Introduction

Mice and rats are live animals, not toys. They can feel hot or cold, hungry or satisfied. They can feel frightened or safe, contented or in pain.

A mouse or rat needs you to look after it all the time. It will cost you extra money each week to feed and look after your pet. Mice may live to be two years old, rats to about three. You will need your parents' permission to have a mouse or rat, as you may need their help to look after it.

Although there are a few small differences, mice and rats need similar care and attention. If you become a responsible mouse or rat owner, you will have a fascinating and attractive pet.

Note to parents

If you decide to have a mouse or rat in your household, please be absolutely sure that it is wanted both by your child and yourself, and that the interest will not wear off after a few weeks.

You must be sure that you are able and willing to supervise its care and well-being for two or three years, and bear the cost of its upkeep during that time. It would be unfair to the animal, to your child and to yourself and family to become unwilling pet owners.

If you buy your mouse or rat from a breeder, there will be many different kinds to choose from. Choose two females unless you want to breed. If you want to keep only one animal, choose a female, as it is easier to tame. The boy in this picture is choosing a mouse.

A variety of rats kept by a breeder. The breeder can advise you on the best kind to keep.

Choosing a mouse or rat

Perhaps you know someone who already keeps mice or rats, and whose doe (female) has had young. Schools which keep mice or rats may also have young for sale.

If you buy your pet from a shop, be sure that it is a clean place with a good reputation for strong, healthy animals.

If you are not sure what kind of mouse or rat to have, visit a show where they are being exhibited. There will be many different kinds of mice and rats there. You will have a chance to meet people who are interested in mice and rats.

8

A healthy rat, like the one in the picture, or mouse has a sleek coat and a firm body. Avoid rats or mice which try to bite or hide in a corner. Never put mice and rats together in the same cage.

It is best to buy a mouse when it is five to six weeks old, and a rat when it is four to five weeks old. Make sure you choose a healthy pet.

Mice and rats should have sleek, smooth coats without any bare patches. The ears should be clean, without any pimples. See that there are no pimples near the base of the tail, either. The eyes should be clean and bright, not watery, half open or sunken.

Mice and rats are very inquisitive. Do not choose a mouse or rat which hides in a corner.

If you are able, buy two pets, as one may be lonely on its own.

Cages with plastic bases and metal tops are the easiest to keep clean and are very light to carry. An exercise wheel attached to the bars is an excellent toy for your pet.

Preparing for your pet

Before you collect your mouse or rat, you must prepare a place in which it can live. You will need to buy a cage made of hard wood, metal or plastic. Pet shops and stores have several kinds of cages for mice and rats.

You can also use a rabbit hutch or a glass fish tank. If you decide to use a fish tank, paint the back panel of the tank black on the outside to cut down some of the light.

Rats and mice are very active, so you must let them have as much space as

If you decide to keep your pet in a wooden cage, check there are no small holes or cracks through which the mouse or rat could gnaw and so escape.

possible. The size of the cage will depend on the number of animals you keep. Allow 900 sq cm (1 sq ft) of floor space for one mouse, and 1800 sq cm (2 sq ft) for one rat. A cage 45 × 25 × 23 cm (18 × 10 × 9 in) high, is suitable for two mice or one rat.

The cage must be strong and dry without any sharp edges on the inside which will hurt the animal. There must not be any holes or cracks which the mouse or rat could make bigger with its sharp teeth, and so escape. Bars must be close together, or the wire mesh

Use heavy earthenware food bowls which your pet will be unable to tip over. Buy enough food for the first few days.

very fine, so that the creature cannot squeeze through.

Mice and rats do not like a lot of light. Do not put their cage near a window or in bright sunlight.

The mouse or rat will need some covering for the floor of the cage. You can use wood shavings, peat or cat litter. You will also need to buy hay for bedding.

If you want to put your pet outdoors, keep the cage on a shelf in a dry shed. Always keep the cage in a sheltered place off the floor. If you want to keep both mice and rats, do not put them in the same cage. You can keep them in cages next to each other, however.

A plastic box makes a good carrying container. Put some hay and a little food in the bottom of the box for the journey home. Go home as quickly as possible so as not to upset your new pet too much. Keep the container level as you carry it.

Taking your pet home

When you go to collect your mouse or rat, take a strong container, such as the cage or a plastic box, in which to carry it home. Do not take a cardboard box, as the mouse or rat will quickly nibble its way out.

Put some hay in the bottom of the container and see that the top is fastened securely. If you take a plastic, wooden or metal box, punch tiny holes in the lid. Do not make the holes too large, for mice and rats can squeeze through very small spaces.

When you buy your pet find out its sex, its age and what it is used to eating.

13

As mice and rats are bulk feeders, see that there is food in the cage at all times. Wash the food bowl every day before putting in fresh food.

Attach the water bottle to the bars of the cage and see that it is low enough for your pet to reach the spout, but not so low that the spout touches the floor. Refill the bottle every day or whenever it is empty.

Food

Mice and rats eat the same kind of food, but rats need more than mice as they are bigger animals. Both mice and rats are "bulk" feeders. This means that they like to eat a little food often, so there should always be food in the cage for them.

Put food into the dish twice a day, in the morning and evening, or once a day in the evening. Remove un-eaten "wet" food from the cage each day, as it will go bad.

Mice and rats need fresh, clean water to drink at all times. A water bowl will become dirty very easily. A "gravity-flow" water bottle fixed to the cage is best for keeping the water clean.

14

Change the water each day. Mice and rats will also get moisture from fresh fruit and vegetables.

Mice need less than 7 gm ($\frac{1}{4}$ oz) of food each day. Rats need 30–40 gm (1–1$\frac{1}{2}$ oz) per day. Mouse rations for 24 hours could be a 2.5 cm (1 in) cube of wholewheat bread soaked in water, and one teaspoonful of whole oats (heaped if crushed).

Rats and mice eat mainly grain and seed. Give your rat or mouse a specially prepared food mix for hamsters, seed mixture for birds, rolled oats or nuts.

Also give your pet some small pieces of fresh food every day. Green food should be given only two or three times a week, and cheese very sparingly.

Above left
The main part of your pet's diet is grain. You can buy grain in large bags which will last a long time.

Above right
Instead of grain, you can give your mouse or rat a food mix which is prepared specially for hamsters.

Put a layer of litter – about 5 cm (2 in) thick – on the bottom of the cage. Remove wet and dirty litter from the cage every day.

Hygiene

Mice and rats are often thought of as being dirty animals – perhaps because they live in dirty places. In fact, mice and rats spend much of their time washing themselves. This is called self-grooming.

Mice and rats usually use one part of their cage – often a corner – as their toilet. Use wood shavings, peat or cat litter to soak up the dampness from the floor of the cage. Spread the litter about 5 cm (2 in) deep. Cleaning will be easier if the cage has a pull-out tray.

It is very important to keep your pet's cage clean. A dirty cage can make your pet ill, and it will smell bad too.

Some cages have a tray at the bottom which slides out. Remove the soiled litter first. Then the tray will slide out easily for cleaning.

Before cleaning the cage, take the mouse or rat out and put it into a safe place. A spare cage, a glass bowl or a show cage can be used, or a strong wooden box if it has a secure lid with air holes. Put a little hay and some food into the bottom of the container.

Take out all the old food, and the food dish. Unclip the water bottle. Remove all the old bedding and soiled litter. Put all the old litter and bedding into a paper bag or newspaper and throw it away.

Scrape out the difficult corners of the cage with a paint scraper or a piece of old cutlery. Then brush out the loose particles.

Put the dirty litter and old food into a plastic bag or a large sheet of newspaper, and throw it away.

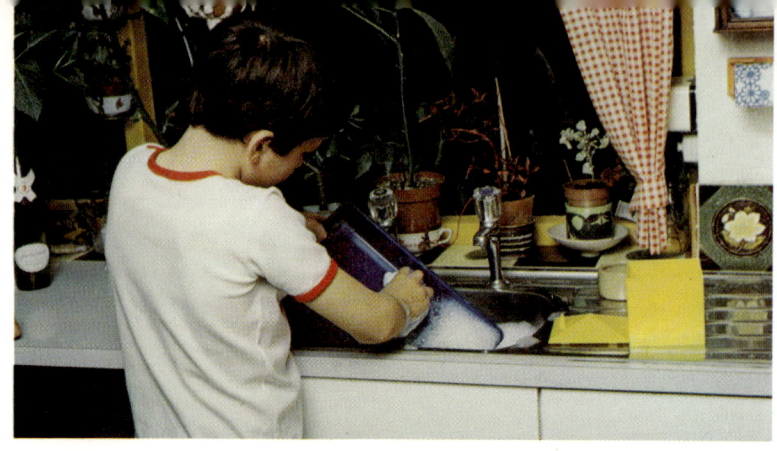

Wash the cage in plenty of soap – washing-up liquid is suitable – and hot water. If you add a disinfectant, check that it is safe for animals.

When the cage has been dried thoroughly, put back all the things your pet needs – fresh food, litter and bedding, and its toys.

Wash the cage with hot soapy water and disinfectant. Make sure that the disinfectant is one which is safe for animals. Wash the food bowls with hot water only as mice, especially, are sensitive to detergents and disinfectants.

Rinse the cage and dry it thoroughly before putting the animal in. A mouse or rat can catch a cold or even pneumonia in a damp cage. Dry a metal or wooden one on top of a radiator or in a low oven.

Put clean litter and bedding in the cage, and place fresh food in a clean dish. Refill the water bottle and clip it on to the cage bars. Removable parts, such as the cage top of a plastic cage, must be fixed securely.

See that your pet has things to play with, otherwise it will become bored. Both rats (like the one in the picture) and mice enjoy running up and down ladders.

Activity

Mice and rats are most lively from early evening onwards. Mice, particularly, love to run and climb. The best kind of cage for a mouse is one built on several levels, with ramps or ladders between the floors. Both mice and rats enjoy playing in an exercise wheel.

Rats are natural burrowers. Put a tube in their cage through which they can run in and out. Rats are more intelligent than mice, so you will be able to teach them simple tricks.

See there is sufficient bedding material for the mice and rats. Hay is best. They like to eat it as well as sleep and play in it.

Rats and mice will be able to exercise themselves in special wheels which can be attached to the bars of the cage. You should also provide a place for your pet to sleep or shelter in. This can be a plastic box, like the one in the picture, a dark glass jar or a tin can (see there are no sharp edges).

Once your pet is used to being handled, play with it every day so that it stays tame.

Rats can be very affectionate once they are tamed, and may even sit on your shoulder.

Handling

Do not handle your pet much at first. Let it get used to your scent and its new home. Do not make sudden or jerky movements when you put your hand into the cage. Move your hand slowly and gently. Offer a few scraps of food to encourage your pet to come towards you. After a week hold the mouse or rat often so that it gets used to being handled.

If your mouse tries to run away while you are holding it, do not squeeze it. Handle your rat very carefully until it gets to know you. A frightened or startled rat may bite you. Once your rat knows you well it will become

20

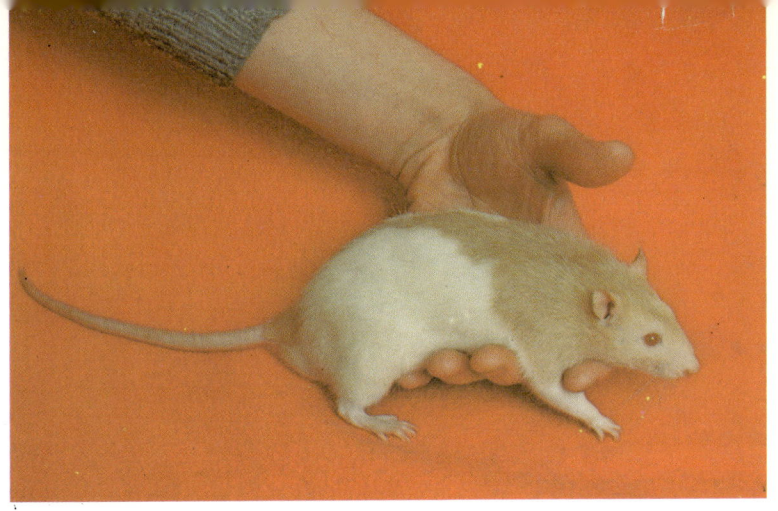

This is the correct way to pick up a rat. Holding its body firmly with one hand, place the rat on your other hand. If your hands are small, hold the rat in both hands.

affectionate, and may even sit on your shoulder.

Pick up a mouse like this. Use your thumb and first finger to pick up the mouse by the base of its tail. Then quickly put it on your other hand. You can steady it there by gently holding the base of its tail. Do not squeeze the mouse, and never pick it up by the middle or the tip of its tail.

Pick up a rat like this. Place one hand over its back, and close your fingers gently under its body. Lift the rat and put it on your other hand. If your hands are small, hold the rat with two hands. Never pick up a rat by its tail, as you could hurt it badly.

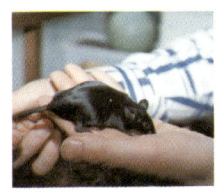

These pictures show the correct way to pick up a mouse. Hold the mouse by the base of the tail and put it on the palm of your hand. Steady the mouse by keeping your fingers on the base of its tail.

21

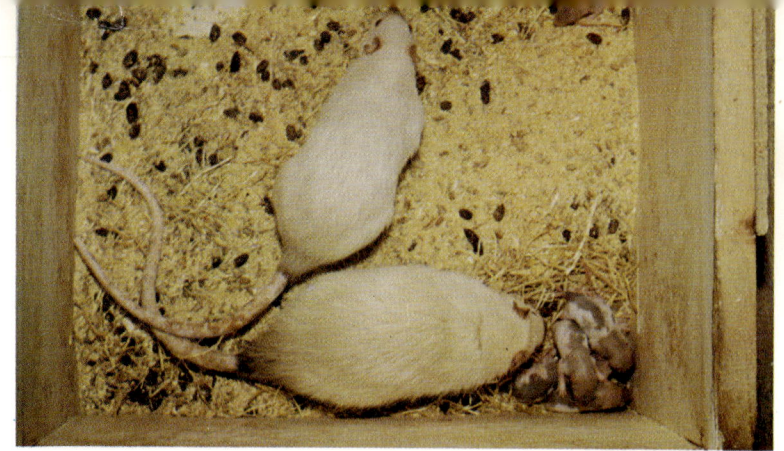

Parent rats with their new-born litter. The cubs feed by suckling milk from the doe. Give the doe bread with milk until the cubs are weaned and are eating solid food.

Determining the sex of a mouse or rat.

Male

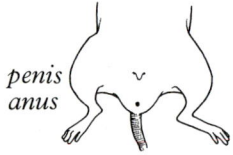

penis
anus

In the male the distance between the anus and penis is about 10 mm ($\frac{1}{2}$ in).

Female

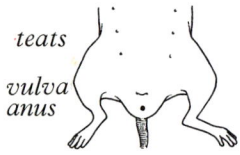

teats
vulva
anus

In the female, the distance between the anus and the vulva is about 5 mm ($\frac{1}{4}$ in).

Breeding

Only breed from your mouse or rat if you are sure you can give the young good homes. You will need extra cages for breeding. Start with two – one for the buck and one for the doe. If you are going to keep the young, you will need a third cage for when they leave their mother. You will need a fourth cage when you separate the males from the females.

For a first mating of mice, the buck should be ten weeks old, and the doe should be twelve weeks old. The best age for mating rats is sixteen weeks.

You can leave a buck rat with a pregnant doe, but not a buck mouse with a pregnant mouse.

This baby rat has not yet grown any hair. When the cubs are weaned – at about three weeks – separate them from the mother. Separate male and female mice after five weeks, and male and female rats after nine weeks.

Young mice are born about twenty days after a successful mating. Young rats are born after twenty-two days. Clean the cage carefully a few days before the litter is due. Put in extra hay with some torn-up paper tissues for the doe to build her nest.

When the litter arrives, do not disturb the nest or touch the cubs (young) for twenty-four hours. There may be six or eight cubs in a litter. Mice and rats are born without hair, and their eyes and ears are closed. Hair grows within three to four days. The eyes and ears open when the cubs are about ten days old. When the cubs are about two weeks old, they will start moving around the cage.

Healthy rats, like the one in the picture, and mice have sleek coats and bright eyes. Occasionally mice and rats get fleas or other insects in their fur. You can buy a special powder to get rid of them.

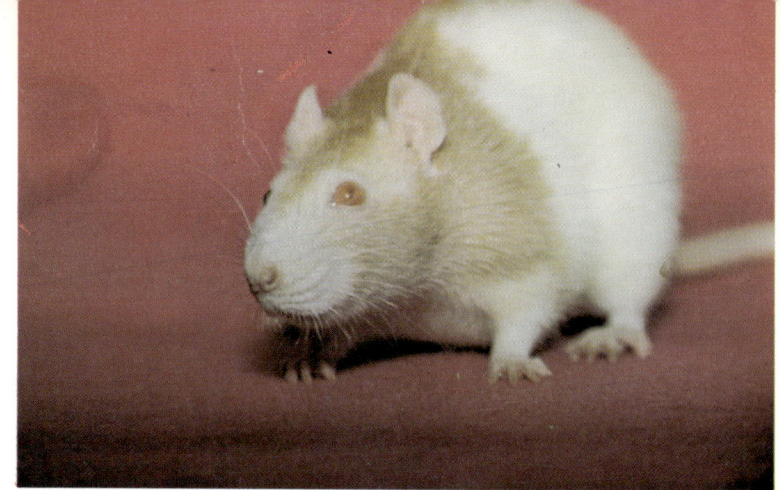

Health and care

Mice and rats are usually healthy creatures, but they may sometimes have upset stomachs or trouble with their breathing. If they catch a cold, it can quickly turn into pneumonia.

When you get your pet, find out who is your nearest vet. If you think that your pet is sick, speak to your vet at once. Do not try to treat the animal yourself.

The signs of a sick animal are:
- runny eyes or ears;
- pimples inside the ear or near the base of the tail;
- a dull coat and dull eyes;
- uneaten food.

Rats, like the one in the picture, and mice spend a great deal of time grooming themselves. They sit up on their hind legs and wash their faces with their front paws.

Mice and rats have long front teeth, called incisors, which grow all the time. If the teeth grow too long, the animal may not be able to eat. A vet can cut the incisors for you. Never try to do this yourself. If you give your pet a wooden block to gnaw on and plenty of hard foods, its teeth will wear down naturally.

As they are naturally clean animals, mice and rats do not need any help from you with their coats. A healthy coat is smooth and sleek, with a nice shine.

When a mouse or rat is sick, its coat will look dull and may feel rough to touch.

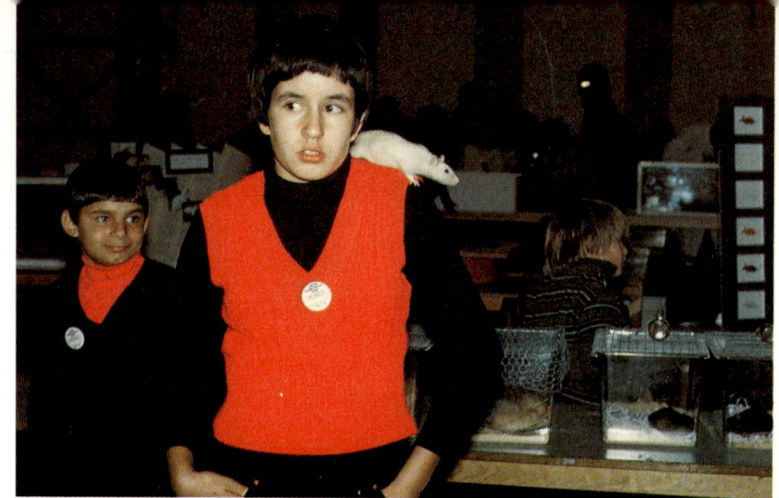

Rat sitting on its owner's shoulder at a show. The owner of the winning animal may receive a trophy, or even some money. Whether you win or not shows are very exciting places. They are also useful because you will be able to meet people who share your interests.

Shows

There are rodent clubs and societies in towns and cities throughout the world. The national organizations hold shows for standard breeds and pedigree mice and rats. A standard mouse and rat must have the correct body shape, coat and markings for its particular variety. Specialist magazines give details of forthcoming shows.

The animals must be in top condition and perfect health to enter a show. They are judged on their general condition and ease of handling.

You can show a pet mouse or rat in its own cage. A standard mouse or rat must be exhibited in a special show

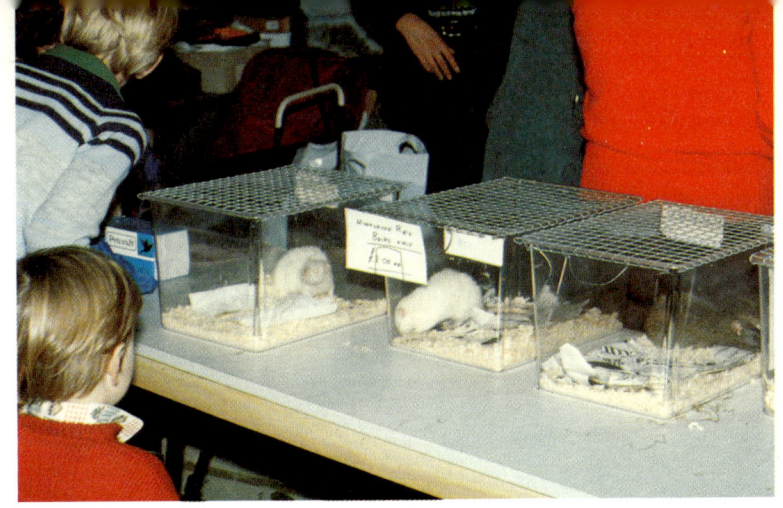

Rats on display at a show. At some shows rats and mice may be on sale.

cage called a "maxey cage". You can buy maxey cages at your local pet store.

During the journey to and from the show, put the cage inside a strong, well-ventilated wooden carrying box.

Before your rat or mouse is judged, you can put it into a special grooming box. This box has fresh hay and sawdust inside it. The animal runs through the sawdust, which dries its fur, and then runs through the hay, which polishes it.

If you gently stroke the animal with a piece of real silk, you will put a shine on its coat. Use a very soft baby brush, to put a shine on long-haired mice.

Dutch mouse.

Fawn mouse.

Agouti mouse.

Varieties of mice

Some varieties of mice are the same shade all over the body. They may be white with pink or red eyes, black, blue, chocolate, red, fawn, champagne, silver, dove or cream. Tan mice have tan undersides but a different shade on the top of the body. Marked mice have patterned coats. The patterns are either spots or patches on white.

Other varieties of mice include cinnamon, chinchilla, sable, silver-brown, silver fawn, pearl, seal point siamese, chocolate himalayan and silver fox.

Himalayan rat.

Varieties of rats

Rats which are the same shade all over the body may be white, black, chocolate, fawn or cream. The capped rat has a white body with a head in a different shade.

Silver fawn hooded rat.

Hooded rats are a variety of marked rats. The body is white and the head is of a different shade, continuing in a stripe down the middle of the back. This stripe is the "hood". Berkshire rats have white on their underside and a different shade on the top of their bodies. The Irish black rat is black all over with white feet.

Black Berkshire rat.

29

Checklist

Before you get your pet you will need
- a cage
- a food dish
- a gravity-flow water bottle
- litter (wood-shavings, peat or cat litter)
- bedding of hay
- food for about a week
- container in which to carry your pet home

Each day
- Change the water
- Feed the mouse or rat once or twice a day
- Remove the soiled litter from the cage
- Check that your pet is lively and healthy

Each week
- Clean the cage completely
- Check that there are enough supplies of litter, bedding and food

When necessary
- Prepare the animal for showing
- Buy a carrying box
- Buy extra cages if you want to breed
- Take the mouse or rat to the vet if it is sick

Glossary

Breeder	person who has many animals which produce young for sale.
Buck	male mouse or rat.
Coat	hair or fur which covers the animal's body.
Cub	young mouse or rat.
Doe	female mouse or rat.
Litter	absorbent material put in the base of the cage to soak up urine and droppings.
Litter	number of young born at the same time to the same mother.
Mating	male and female coming together to have young.
Maxey cage	special cage in which all standard mice must be shown.
Nest	hay or other bedding arranged by the doe in which she has her young.
Standard	ideal body shape, coat, shade and markings for a recognized variety.
Weaning	getting the young used to eating solid food instead of suckling their mother's milk.

Index

activity, 19

bedding, 12, 17, 18, 19
breeder, 8
breeding, 22–23
buck, 8, 22

cage, 11, 12, 19, 22, 23
   cleaning, 16, 17–18
carrying box, 13, 27
clubs, and societies, 26
coat, 9, 24, 25
cubs, 23

dishes, 14, 18
doe, 8, 22

exercise wheel, 10, 19

food, 12, 14–15, 18, 20
food mix, 15

gnawing block, 25
grain, 15
gravity-flow water bottle, 14, 17
grooming, 16, 27
grooming box, 25

handling, 20–21, 26
health and care, 24, 25, 26
housing, 10–12
hygiene, 16–18

illness, 24

litter, 12, 16, 17, 18
litter (young), 23

maxey cage, 27
mouse varieties, 28

nest, 23

outdoor housing, 12

rat varieties, 29

sawdust, 27
seed, 15
self-grooming, 16, 25
sex determination, 22
shows, 8, 26, 27
standard breeds, 26

tail, 9, 24
tank, 10
teeth, 11, 25
toilet area, 16
toys, 19

vet, 24, 25

water, 14, 18
weaning, 23